THE CAGED SOUL

SHIPRA VERMA

Made with ❤ on the Notion Press Platform
www.notionpress.com

Contents

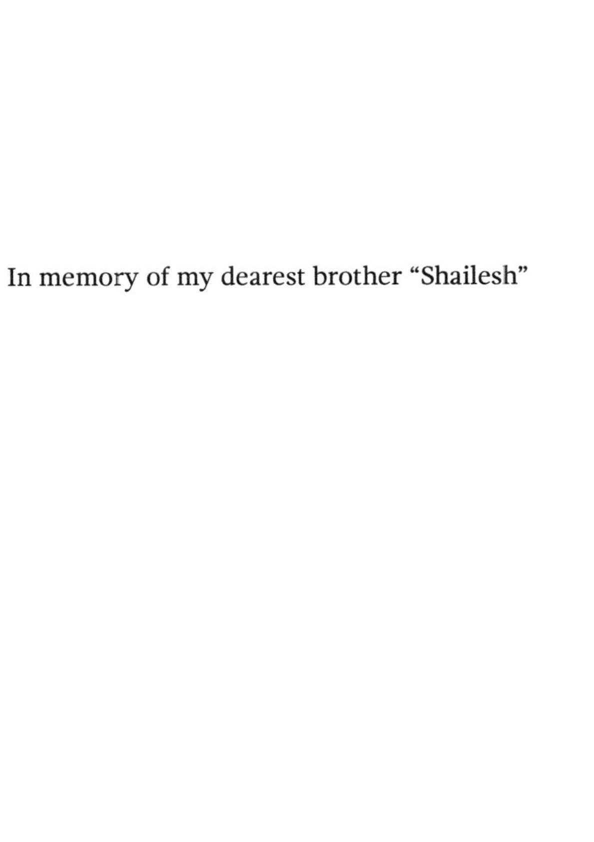

In memory of my dearest brother "Shailesh"

Preface

The year Two Thousand Twenty (2020) was the beginning of a disastrous period of time globally. Before the world got armed enough to combat this newly arrived evil foe called 'corona' or Covid-19, it had already engulfed and engraved its deadly presence all over the world. Like many eternal optimists, my big brother 'Shailesh' along with me, always thought this is not going to catch us! As if we are so pure spirits with such a huge baggage of good deeds that an invisible small little virus is not going to harm us, at least of now and that our time on this earth is still not come. That we have to live a little longer and there are so many things that we still have to do and experience more and therefore, if at all, there is any corona threat or life-challenging disease, we will not be affected by it now. We used to hear news on television and newspapers which said so many lives have been finished, cities are turning into graveyards, the world health organization has proclaimed an emergency which it is incapable of handling, and so on and so forth; but our deadly optimism refused to accept this could ever happen to us!

The Year 2020 and the covid-19 virus then felt bad and humiliated about our optimism and then they first infected one of our family members who was working out in the field with the first mild sting and shook our confidence when the first wave arrived. She was however young and her immunity quite strong, hence she recovered soon. Later on, as soon as the vaccine was developed, she got herself vaccinated first! Shailesh refused to get vaccinated! Twenty-twenty-one:- Jan, Feb, March hardly passed and the crucial phase of his life when his only teenage son cleared the Ninth Class finals and had to start preparations for his Matriculation exams...His son was his only dream as he was a brilliant child but off late was not getting proper care and attention and therefore his percentage was dropping a bit...and the doting father that Shailesh was, vowed to totally focus him about his studies. He started to send his son to a very exceptionally bright teacher with brilliant records for coaching from the First of April 2021. Hardly did he know that the scorching heat would ooze out not only his sweat and blood but also suck out his life out of his body! A little fever, then, cold, cough, loss of appetite...His wife doubted on the 5th... "Are we facing a life threat?" Do these symptoms lead to the death of an energetic and smart person influenced by the energy of Mars who worked non-stop relentlessly even when he was a little sick? But, alas! To the disbelieve of one and all, death bells really started ringing which finally culminated in his death on Amavasya, 11th April. Did he purposely neglect his health? Did he grab the opportunity to die? Why?

Why would he do so? He was such a passionate and loving soul, eternally optimistic even when he was totally surrounded by negative forces all around him? He was the guiding inspiration for so many souls who asked his help and guidance and he always rewarded them all with the booty of positivity, filled their hearts and minds with Hope and optimism!

Such thoughts kept on pestering me for days and weeks and months until and unless I decided to sit down and pen those thoughts and questions on tenth of June 2021, which coincided with his second monthly date of demise, the dark, deadly Amavasya (No Moon)! And since then, I decided to write, I honestly admit, it was a very, very tough deed to do so, indeed. All those emotions, experiences, memories, scenes started coming alive once again. While writing, often I used to drown in the volley of tears which used to start pouring out as soon I started to frame the sentences and my laptop would become wet so much so that I had to stop typing and shut down my system. Then for hours and hours I would remain unstable flowing down his memory lane like a turbulent sea caught in a fierce storm! I would turn on to family and friends, my sisters, brother, husband for emotional support and to help me out of this crisis. Here and there some bits of pieces which somehow I managed to pen down haphazardly on some days and dates, I have brought out together in this memoir which I have named "The Caged Soul." It is a real contradiction that a person like my big brother who believed in the freedom of every soul was himself reduced to a caged soul in his life and who freed himself by the merciful and non-hypocritical truthful element Death. I share the pain and grief of all such wonderfully blessed and divine good souls who are never understood when they are alive and never treated properly by anyone, rather they are 'mistreated' by one and all!

This memoir may awaken all those people who unknowingly misbehave with good souls and their ignorance, many a times becomes one reason for the precious loss of such persons who are beneficial for not just their own families, but for the entire world. Many lives are lost every day, every moment and every second all over the world. As is said that, 'Death is inevitable!' We all are in the death train, yet we believe the time is not yet come for ourselves and for those who are close to us. But the inexplicable fact remains that when is the time of death. So, I feel that, according to me, we should all try to live our lives by such a conduct as if we are to die the next moment and so, never should we misbehave with any living soul.

Personal stories of a common man do not account for any status in literature or rather the society, I am very well aware of the fact. Yet, I wish to highlight the memories of a soul who is deeply missed by anyone and everyone who even for once came into his contact due to his extra-ordinary, selfless and humane nature, which is almost an extinct *virtue* in today's world. When such a person departs, the void he creates is never ever filled and the only way to move away is by encompassing his beautiful thoughts and memories; to remember the small and big lessons in our day-to- day life which can help us to make a more fulfilled and accomplished person. Many of my learned friends do not agree with me at all and they ask me to **"forget and move ahead"** but let me be very frank to say that "forgetting him is like forgetting myself"...My father, mother and brother have only physically left this earth..I am attached to them since my birth and their memories are safe in my system till I am alive. I owe all my knowledge, values and cultural heritage to them. Sometimes, unconsciously I do things the way they used to do and I become quite surprised how did I do something I never knew earlier. Then, upon deep meditation I get the answer that this was the way they used to do. Therefore, my wholesome entity also belongs partly to my father, mother and my big brother, Shailesh!

CHAPTER ONE

AMAVASYA (NO MOON)

The Tenth of June, 2021! There is gloom of Amavasya (no moon) and the sun is also eclipsed. Nature is revengeful and merciless. It is shutting off the two main sources of light we depended since we opened our eyes on this earth! My *amavasya* and *eclipses* are not for a day--- it has been continuing for years...though sometimes I used to steal a bit of light here and there when I Iooked at the stars!

Exactly **two months** have passed and Amavasyas extend for couple of days rather than few hours or just a single day, since the light of my being, my brother *Shailesh* departed from his earthy cage! That was the longest *Amavasya* probably I witnessed in my life. 11th April, 2021 was the *Chaitra Amavasya*. I saw the Sun enveloped in darkness and exactly at the time when diyas are lit and incenses burned in every home, my lighthouse was turned off! I saw the light of my house, my 'big brother' finally close his eyes. A person who never used to sleep and even while sleeping his big eyes used to be open, how could those eyes close forever? I was not able to believe it at any cost. I thought that he must be playing a little prank on me.

A few minutes before he caught my hands and asked me a promise that I will never leave him alone; now how could he leave all of us and leave me **alone**!

Alone!!

He said he lived a very lonely life although he was surrounded by so many family members! The journey onwards also he had to take alone. He might have mastered loneliness but I was so naïve for this lonely journey further on this earth. Oh! How desperately I wished to go along with him and wished to spend all my life and after-life also with him who was my true soul-mate, my brother, my father and mother, my friend, philosopher, guide, my intellect and my brains, my heartiest and closest person in my life after my father! I think he loved me more than I could and therefore, merciful/merciless death snatched him from me!

Tenth of June, year 2021. In India, this date to be the *amavasya* of *jyeshtha* month. This is a day when women adorn their bridal attires and pray to the almighty god for the well being of their husbands and cool them with a hand-made fan from the scorching heat of the summer noon and light lamps under the banyan tree in the no-moon night. The banyan tree is known for its long life and every married woman wishes that her husband lives longer than her! Today, my brother's young wife can't bloom with the bliss of marital glory in the typical, traditional Indian way, I feel so helpless to think about her who religiously observed the rituals for the past fifteen years, and she has to withdraw suddenly from so many festivities because of the miserable incident. Ever since the past few years, I haven't been observing festivals and fasting the way I used to observe them earlier as my belief systems have been somewhat modified. Many rituals which I was stringent about following them in their purest format, I am not at all finicky and particular about them anymore! Watering plants is religion or say 'Dharma' for me! So not just banyan and tulsi, but I water all the big and small trees, even bushes and grass around me!

Nature has its own unique way to indicate and forecast the events which are going to happen. The Sun, the Moon directly influence the Earth. But when we are young and surrounded by our parents and siblings enjoying the warmth and protection of love and care, it seems that the entire solar system is in our control and the changing phases of the moon or the solar, lunar eclipse does not have any effect on us. But when we have lost them, even the slightest movement of the celestial bodies start affecting us heavily. Why is it so? Do we become more sensitive and prone to these invisible energies and are exposed more as we do not have the physical covering of our protectors? This I have experienced that on full moon and no moon (amavasya) days even if I am unaware of the particular day, yet I have a feeling of uneasiness and my head becomes heavier for no reason which exhibits fatigue and migraine symptoms until that phase passes out. I must say that my fearless self has become now fearful of particularly the no moon (amavasya) days of every month. I keep praying especially on those days that no untoward incident happens in my home as well as the whole world. I think it may be a way for the higher authorities of the universe for us to realize that we are but tiny living beings and our lives are actually being controlled by a force much powerful than our wildest imagination. The rest of the days our physical human form makes us believe that we can create innumerable wonders on this earth with our might and insight. What can human beings not do after all? Since aeons and aeons we feed ourselves with this '*pleasure thought*' of our might but we all end up in fright when the realization dawns how petty we are and how huge is the creation and Creator!

CHAPTER TWO

RAINDROPS

My eternal soul is ever struggling for luminescence. I get up early morning and see the *raindrops* have already watered all my seeds, seedlings, the grasses, bushes and the big trees... all have their leaves wet. There's not been a single day when I have risen from my bed without my big brother's thought, I fondly called him "Bhai"! He was Bablu for my mother and father, Shailesh for his classmates, friends, neighbours, the shopkeepers etc. "Bhai" for we four sisters and younger brother "Chapu" and Bhai Mama for nieces Tisha and Tunmun, Papa for his son Mist and twin daughters Yashi and Yashmini and Bade Papa for Soumya!

I cannot say whom he loved less because his exuberance and love irradiated with each and every human interaction. He was an ocean of love one can say! Giving away all his life and never expecting from anyone... that was Shailesh! He set an example on the footsteps of our father Dr. U.K. Verma who selflessly served the sick without anything in return, and who even didn't write his doctor title and remained simply Mr. U.K.Verma, Stenographer giving his extraordinary services at Central Fuel Research Institute, Dhanbad. Shailesh inherited all the genetic as well as socio-philosophic traits of Papa! Our grandfather was the richest zamindar of a village Radhaur, Sitamarhi in Bihar. During his time all the marriages of the daughters of the village would be hosted by him. The festivities would go on for two to three...you guessed it days? No no, it was two to three months! *Shehnaai* was played by none other than Ustad Bismillah Khan and musicians and artists of such highest grade used to come and perform. The sheer grandeur and elegance of his personality would attract all from the *'class to the mass'*. In my childhood I heard stories about the herd of elephants, horses and his big cattle stock of cows, goats and sheep he had and also I remember when I was ten years old there was a strong room which was filled with gold and silver ornaments just like I read stories of Kings and Queens! But my father, the youngest child of the rich household went out to fetch his own destiny with hard work and left the entire property for his elder brother and his son. Shailesh was eldest son but he was a true Karm-Yogi. The 'Bhagwad Gita' was his rule book he followed sternly the Shloka-"*Karmaneyavadhikaaraste Maaphaleshu Kadachan*"...just do your duty and don't expect the fruits! He knew that "Nothing is mine", that he is just an instrument to do 'seva' (service) towards his family, friends and all who came in his contact without any iota of return expectations. He was the representation of very strong masculine powers as well as the soft feminine virtues of care and concern for the entire world! I was "***Shipra***", his closest sister just two years younger and the bonding was so strong that the world became envious of such strong bonding in this age. And the sad part was both of us were not rich materialistically! We couldn't become rich in terms of money but when I decided to quit Mumbai due to my long lonely life, then I decided to come to him and only him because for me, he was the richest kin I had! Many of my cousins mocked his unemployed status and pressurized me to come and stay with them but I refused to leave my richest brother (emotionally, spiritually and physical strength of a Martian). I left a nice job in Mumbai and packed off one fine rainy day in 2019 only to enjoy the care and love of family only a few months before the Covid-19 started to appear. Six months was the only time period I could enjoy his closeness and nearness and it only made my bond further more stronger with him and made me admire, adore and respect him to all the greater extent than I already did earlier!

As I mentioned earlier, to many souls this brother-sister bonding was unbearable. To add to their envy was the fact that we both were unemployed at that time. I was struggling to find something suitable work/business as well as he was thinking along the same lines for himself and his family. We both were the unluckiest in terms of government job, He even won the case from the court but still couldn't get compassionate employment in CFRI; I started contractual job in CFRI but my marriage spoiled everything! The unending struggles we both faced pursuing for jobs, livelihood till this fifty years of age is difficult to describe. The pains and hurt he experienced was maximum; he had a wife and three small kids and although I understood his pain, I couldn't do much for him, rather I leaned on to him whenever I felt low. I did realize his heart and mind, intensely, as I myself experienced all those in my life, but all the other family members and the society never understood or helped him; rather they always ridiculed and blamed him all the while especially because he was a man!!

He was always available with his heart and soul and body to help out others but nobody ever came out to help him, even always denied his rightful rights each and every time! He worked hard, he took risks, he took hard, rough journeys sometimes without food and water for days he gained a lot of experience with which he further served his fellow beings and family, but there was no one who really loved and cared for him. A highly positive soul was surrounded, rather "caged" by only negative vibes and vicious thinking for him. And these were the souls for whom Shailesh always thought to help and assist in some or other way. True that someone said, "You get everything in this world, but not from whom you expect"... He didn't expect too but at least he deserved some positive thoughts for him rather than abuses and filthy words all the time. Sometimes I wonder God has made so many things free; and love is so easy to give, why we all only wish to receive love and fear to give love to even our family members? Wealth, intellect, charms, or any charisma cannot override the power of love and yet we are so miserly to give it. I see people even sometimes give away some money/ materialistic things but they will refrain to give love... They just cannot love! And treading this journey of life Shailesh became the "Why worry' syndrome! He kept on preaching to everyone- "Why Worry"? But this was probably only for the guidance and help to others. On his part, himself, he never used to sleep properly. Whole night he used to be awake and contemplation was his fixed routine as of! When the whole world would be engrossed in deep sleep he used to simply sit in the chair and talk to the dark shadows of fear. When we were a bit younger, i.e. in our thirties, then 'Akinchan Kunj' in Dhanbad was famous for its surprise parties in the middle of the night, may be 12 a.m. one or two which was a rare event for a small town like Dhanbad which sleeps soon after night falls. This was because he would get up in the middle of the night and start calling out to all the family members that he is hungry and going to eat nice delicious food. This was a prompt for all of us because he was the best cook artist and could cook wonders in no time, as well as he was a foodie who loved to eat classic food. So, he was free to express those days and we used to eat, cook and enjoy along with him. These extended dinners will be a thing of only memories and dreams now!

After mother's demise in 2015, Shailesh was completely broken from inside. He almost stopped living for himself but his infallible smile and his energetic hearty welcome never let anybody doubt of what was going on deep inside him. He was withdrawing, retreating within his shell like the tortoise but he remained the lion heart still on his face! Midnight surprise parties ended as he couldn't gather the courage to "disturb" any family member in the mid of the night to share the joy and excitement. Therefore, the family members enjoyed their 'rest' while he started to suffer his 'loneliness' amidst all of them.

He always gathered the time somehow to call me over the phone daily when I was away from 'Akinchan Kunj' home. His prime motto used to be that I should not feel "alone", but he suffered silently without complain. To him, every person was his own part, so to whom to complain about whom? He humbled down and took all the blame upon himself for the failures of all others. He gave credits and appreciation to the successes to others for whom he toiled day and night, but I guess some kingmakers die in oblivion like him. All his friends who became successful due to him shall never ever pay any tribute to him. All the most they can do is to remember him some times when they get caught in certain complicated problems. He was their "Quick Fix" who had the immediate solutions for all their major problems.

CHAPTER THREE

SEEKING GUIDANCE

I couldn't write for few days due to my mental and physical weaknesses. Emotionally too, I am drained out without Shailesh! Therefore, I sit in front of his (Shailesh's) photograph which I had clicked recently in the month of February when he was going to attend the marriage ceremony of a neighbour's daughter! I ask his photograph to give directions to my brain and to speak up to my soul...(since he is now in spirit and soul form) he is definitely able to communicate so, I believe. But there is silence! Only my mind is chattering and rustling-hustling about to reach nowhere! Oh! What a havoc I've created in myself? All who know me used to ask and seek advices from me were the ones consoling me and reminding me that I was "guru" to so many of them. How could they understand that my real guru was my brother whom I used to seek advice for all my people who comforted in me for their advice and direction from time to time! I switch over to my phone, start checking out the innumerable whatsapp messages and my facebook; then of course I start my singing app *starmaker* and sing a couple of songs. And even when I am singing I remember my brother Shailesh's words... he used to say that I am really gone crazy singing all the time. When I was a teenager, he once put a bet on me if I could be silent without singing for even ten minutes he would give me ten paisa.. (Ten paise would fetch ten orange juice toffees that time)! And till I grew old and got married, I never won the ten paisa bet. By now he had understood me that singing and poetry cannot be taken away from me if I am to be happy and therefore he allowed me to sing to my heartful. He told me regarding my earnings and finances---"God shall provide for you till he calls you back, till that time Eat, drink and be merry and live life to the fullest;" is what he used to always say particularly to me!

Meanwhile, he used to discuss his dreams and plans with me and suddenly he used to sink down into deep thoughts of how and when will things happen. His wife NM could only envy our brother-sister bonding and tried to create as many misunderstandings and hatred in his mind against us but all the time she failed to do so and used to get herself all the more frustrated! I completely empathized with my sis-in-law and understood her as she was quite younger to me in age as well as her marital experience! She couldn't understand her husband, my brother too, obviously, cause she had totally different upbringing where she was trained to see for her own self first and my brother was always looking towards the needs of others..., be it family members, friends, neighbors or relatives; even strangers would choose him for respite and shelter and food and care. He was such a helpful person! His each and every breath was for generosity purpose, not that he didn't have his own needs, desires and aspirations! But he always kept his own needs behind and tried to fulfill the wishes of all his people.

'People'--- I wished to put loved ones instead but then second thoughts started haunting me.

Questions and questions started arising! –

Do we equally love the person who loves us dearly?

Do we have any idea of how much a person loves us?

Even if we are aware of the person's love for us, does each of us reciprocate equally?

Why does a person keeps loving in spite of innumerable times of rejection, abuse and misbehavior of the loved one?...

What strengthens the integrity of love?

What and how does love become lesser?

How to explain our love for others?

Questions are being asked by Tunmun daily (three year old niece):

1. Bhai Mama please tell, why did you go?
2. Where are you now?
3. What are you doing there? Please be very happy wherever you are!
4. Why did you not eat when you were hungry?
5. How and when can we see you again?
6. If you had stayed with us, you would not die.
7. You called me 'jhingri' which I didn't like. Does that mean you will never call me?

(19th, june 2021)

CHAPTER FOUR

Daily Chores

Clouds have covered the morning sky. By the time I am done with my usual morning chores, have my bath and puja the clouds have further emboldened by the heavy water droplets they were holding whole night and by the time I sit down to have my breakfast the showers start falling. My sister who is the eldest sibling starts talking about his daily routine! How he used to be awake since 3.00 a. m. morning and by 6.00 a. m. he used to wake Alka who was addressed as "Chotka didi" by all of the Verma family siblings! He would guide her as to what would be the breakfast menu, the lunch and also the dinner. Preparing, cutting, washing the vegetables for a family of ten was also a big task. Then the cleaning, brooming, mopping, washing of both clothes and the dishes.... It seemed endless job. He also had to see to all the external work, paying the bills, filling the house/ property taxes, the school fees of his three children, the electricity/water etc. charges, the motorcycle/ car licenses renewals...shopping, fetching ration/ fruits/ vegetables/ fish etc. Then he thought of investments and maintenance of his Akinchan Kunj home, the plastering and whitewashing, the electric fittings to be repaired, the water pipes to be replaced...etc. He also fulfilled all the social obligations; being there for whosoever needed his physical and mental presence and advice! Whatever he did, he did with totality with perfection.! If any other member would do a simple brooming it would be such that he would have to do it all again because he aimed perfection in each and every little work! When he would sit for his daily worship, it would be not less than an hour and half whereas when we did it would be for ten minutes only! Patience, tolerance are virtues no doubt, but Shailesh had overcome his very existence to take these to a totally different level. Perhaps, this was what not liked and understood by everyone and he started to become the subject of loathing due to his extraordinary ingenuity.

He was never understood within his own family or anyone else! Being the elder brother, elder son he had only duties to perform and no rights to receive love or respect. Only the blames and shames were his rewards. Gains and fame for which he worked hard were granted to others. He was *Jyeshtha* born,* born with responsibilities and responsibilities since his earliest childhood and had to be the *father-figure* for all the youngsters.

24th June

Since past few days I keep wondering about the definition of true success. Who is a successful person? Who is a great human being? I am made to believe that any one who has gathered ample of wealth, fame and materialistic achievements within a certain age is a successful man. That means every boy has to earn money so much as to build a house, run the household and cater to the needs of his society...Right? A girl has to be in the care of her parents first and then marry and be in the care of the spouse and his family for all her needs! By and large as per rule, all boys have to be rich! So when we look at the unemployment figures what do we understand? That the rules of the society cannot be fairly applied and there will be imbalances in the society.

'S' fought this imbalance in his daily life like many others who might be facing the similar situation in the world. By keeping a very positive mind he combated through negativity all around him. He struggled to live a decent life but never got so. The struggles and challenges only became more and more severe and tougher as he grew up. He learned the art of cooking when his friends did not even know to boil a cup of milk too. And so he went on to pursue a career in Hotel management out of Dhanbad at eighteen. He travelled and learned from whosoever he came in contact from Patna, Gaya, Siliguri, Assam, Kolkata, Delhi, Mumbai, Goa and the more he stayed away earning his bread, the more worrisome my mother became! Once she came to know his whereabouts when he was working in a five star hotel in Gaya and she landed there all of a sudden with all the graduation books and asked him to return home and complete his graduation course. So he returned home and successfully passed his Bachelor degree, but again tensions started fuming up for his unemployment which finally ended by seeking the job of a Club Manager at Tata company. The youngest sister Iti got the prize for brother's job. The other three of us were just happy that now our elder brother is employed and we can raise our heads and say to our college friends and neighbors that our brother didn't become an engineer or a doctor or a scientist (the most coveted jobs then in that place) but yes he has achieved something which was unique and nobody in our locality had pursued hotel management career at that time.

He was a brilliant manager, a great crisis manager, a sea of innovative ideas always floating in his sharp mind which he could apply whenever the right time would arise. But unfortunately, his brilliance was not liked by the egotist colleagues wherever he worked. Each time whenever he used to save the organization from a crisis or emergency situation, he would be fired away for his excellence.

"Employers do not need excellent employees, they need only the employees who are average."

This is a really pathetic situation which has arisen due to the long, long years of British slavery where Indians only worked for average posts and minimum wages. After the British the Indian bosses applied the same for Indian workers...what an evolvement...Huh! More or less I experienced the same way and me and my brother were always in and out of jobs due to our nature or call it "Karma"! Our dedicated hard work and sincerity would not be appreciated and we would be shown out of the door with due respect every other time. This was the story outside, but even when we started getting stabilized and settling in some job, our family would show up such a huge need and crisis that we had to leave everything and be by their side to take care for them.

Father suffered from rheumatic heart disease which he first contracted when he was only fourteen years old. When I was in my Second grade he had a by-pass heart operation and by the time I was in my crucial Tenth standard he was severely ill and had to undergo an open heart operation. Before he was leaving for All India Institute of Medical Sciences, New Delhi, he summoned 'me' and my brother and explained what we should do in case he didn't return home from Delhi.

The alarm bells of someone close to us dying was first heard by me and my brother that time.! We had no choice but to become further mature before our friends and peers!

My heart overwhelms while I walk down those memory lanes and many a time I stop writing and keep contemplating for days and days. The "Why, What, Who, How, When etc. questions keep on haunting me and giving nightmares. I can't sleep for nights properly, in fact I never had a sound peaceful sleep for years and years I think barring a few occasions. And this is not the restless mind of a poet and author, rather it is the restless mind of a common man who has to struggle for his basic needs from day one to his last breath! Shailesh resonated with my mind, being the elder brother, the elder son and no brothers to share and understand his views, thoughts and feelings he was eternally restless, although he appeared calm, serene, balanced, happy, thoughtful, energetic and a lot more positive person to the whole world. The one and only negativity which engulfed him and his life was that he was jobless after a certain point of time. He was unemployed, his business ventures all flopped, his investments got burnt, he got cheated in many of them and ultimately he was reduced to Maa's *pension and tension!* His management skills helped Maa to pretty well manage the household with all the prestige for which it was known since father's time. For example, there was never a chance when a guest arrived and he would have to leave the house without proper food and snacks and tea. Even a stranger who would accidently come in our arena would be given proper attention, care and refreshments before he reached his actual destination. That was the trend continued by Shailesh when all his rich neighborhood would hardly entertain with even a glass of water. So, when the Trimurti

Apartments came up next to Akinchan Kunj, Shailesh organized for a "*Devi-Jagran*" and *Hawan* for the entire society and all his rich neighbors too came with all their families to have the '*Prasad-bhog*' and seek the blessings, but none of them contributed in the manner they could have either physically, emotionally or financially. Shailesh made each of the flat owners feel home in their new locality- that was the greatest thing about him. Why I say it to be the greatest thing because how much he ssstried to make and feel each stranger homely, he was been continuously pushed out of his own home after he got married and later on when younger brother's wife arrived in the household. Now these two new ladies had all the rights of the house, they were the owners and he was just the caretaker, the watchdog, the servant, the manager laboring for all the tasks and enjoying a third degree status in his own home! What a tragedy! The garden which he had nurtured with his sweat and labour and love was snatched away from him and he couldn't complain to anybody. There came a time when he lost the rights to even plant a small flower tree in his own garden. The reason I decided to write this memoir was that this is not the sole story of Shailesh and there are many, many successful people who undergo the same casualties and are prey to untimely death and I can't find any solution to this unfairness till now! I am not a person to hold grudges against anyone and I respect the feelings of everyone. I think the society needs to change its pattern of thinking a lot.

As I grow older my only prayers for the younger generation is not that they earn stinkingly rich money or fame or educational degrees; but that each and everyone should be blessed by **GOOD LUCK**! And what do I mean by good luck is Simplicity, love, care, trust, affection, sensitivity and a hell lot of human-ness! (Humanity).

It's the 31st of July, 2021...

About three and a half months after Shailesh left his mortal body his belief and aspiration that his sister, Shipra would be finally settled down at her in-laws house is realized. Shipra reached her in-laws place after her husband finally took the initiative; but all this couldn't happen until he was alive! He was awfully resented for being so good and sensitive towards his sister that the sister's husband and his family couldn't tolerate this and ill-treated, abandoned her for as long as they could. So, is it that a person becomes much more powerful in the spirit and soul form, rather than when he/she is in their physical body? The question haunts me!

Why could not this simple event which could give him a great amount of happiness and satisfaction happen earlier when he was alive? Was he a threat to the in laws because of his sheer charismatic personality? Or it was a case of unnecessary ego clash? Or it was simply the unchangeable/ undeniable cruel destiny? I am speechless on this point.

The 10[th of] August 2021

I am at Saharsa, arrived finally after a long struggle as per Shailesh's dream and aspirations when he is no more physically present in this world! My stinkingly rich in-laws never provided me even my basic needs and I am still struggling for my basic rights here. Shailesh used to often say that "you have to finally go to your in-laws place and ask for your rights". If you were married in that family you deserve the rights of a daughter-in-law and you will have to demand now, because even if you have no materialistic ambitions and you wish to become a 'Buddha', then also first you have to become Prince Siddhartha and live the royal life. For almost your whole life you have been working hard for your survival, now it's time for you to enjoy real life"...was what he used to keep saying! My brother and I loved people; and we found all the rest of the world loving property! He was 'King of Hearts' and master of human communications. He was a person who could understand anybody's heart and mind even without a single utterance of any word. He would go out of his way to reach out and help people of any social strata, especially the poor and needy! They reciprocated with further increased respect and gratitude for him but destiny didn't give him material wealth in cash!

15th Aug, 2021

Sometimes I worry how much does it take for a so called very highly educated, exceptionally famous and successful person to understand and behave correctly with another person! Shailesh was bestowed with supernatural powers to understand and rightly behave with each and every person who came his way. He was the best friend of someone's grandfather, father, son and grandson alike! Each individual used to share their problems with only Shailesh and he could come out with the best remedy for each one of them; he could make everyone happy in the end. Someone has aptly said- "what is that one thing that you can give even if you don't have it yourself?" And yes, it is love and happiness and respect! Although he was the unluckiest person who was deprived of all his rights and happiness, yet he showered and kept showering his affection and love to the classes and masses alike. In fact, he loved the labor and the deprived, more than anyone. When the transgender community group used to visit in the neighborhood whenever there was a happy occasion, they all used to knock his door first and he used to take due care of them and never let them leave without having food or snacks.

He was special! Not just because I am his sister, but to whosoever who ever had a chance to enjoy his presence even for a while, they all will endorse this fact.

"For million years nature awaits patiently,

Sometimes such rare gems are born!"

17th Sept, 2021

Slowly, I can feel the magic that Shailesh can create. Good things start happening from all those arenas which almost looked impossible before. He is badly missed on all the festivals and occasions while the shades of life, color and happiness continue their penetration into the lives of all others and specially we siblings. His wishes have become divine blessings for all of us. We are climbing the social ladder, owing our own personal houses, growing in our almost dead careers and having the love and care of our families! Our endless struggles to live a proper life suddenly gets smoothening out now and he isn't there to witness them all. Had he been alive, he would have been the happiest on earth for each of our simple achievements but nevertheless, he is there within us, for sure! Only when we become all inclusive with him, is the time that we actually enjoy our lives!

18th Oct: This is the date when Shailesh descended down on earth before me, his birthday; and when I opened my eyes he was my two-year old big brother! He was the first son and never could he really become anything but big... So he had big responsibilities, big, larger than life dreams, big thoughts, great deeds, great feelings and emotions, in fact he was a great person. The only single thing he did never have was a great fate! I know all will argue with me that do not account your failures to fate. All those people who have amassed a lot of material possessions and property and wealth, their showy social status their high lifestyle would attribute their successes to their own wit and wisdom and hard work or rather smart work. Shailesh couldn't become rich in terms of material wealth and probably this was the major failure which enflamed his life and almost consumed and finished him! After he got married, things started to become from bad to worse. Although he had a big heart, he was not blessed by big money. Deprived of huge ancestral property, betrayed for a rightful government job, cheated by his entrepreneur friends who cracked the jackpot with his help and guidance, ignored by all family members, abused and ill-treated by immediate family members... Shailesh still could remain the warm, loving saintly human who kept smiling and laughing on his face, although his heart kept bleeding in intense pain. The biggest pain was he could share his pain with no one, but each and everyone would come to him to vent out their pain and take a slice of comfort out from him. He was master of comforting people, of studying their feelings, understanding their pain, and wise fully preaching the simplest methods to tackle and come out of unpleasant experiences. On the other hand, he had no one to resolve his own pain. He was such a good friend that he was talked about and loved by his friends, but they came to him for their problems and none could do anything concrete for him in his lifetime. He was dangerously positive and optimistic although and kept saying there is light, there is hope, that this darkness will not stay forever but the cruelest fate he inherited, never let him see the good times and good days what we know.

Diwali- Bhai-Dooj-Chhatth2021

There is never a day when I do not miss him. Festivals are no more festivals; no more fun without him. Deepawali is dark in spite of the thousand lamps and lights lit all around. I am re-joined with my husband and am wearing the brightest red Kanjivaram saree presented by him yet, the gloom of his departure persists. I have prepared a water candle, made small rangoli, and lit a small diya in front of my newly brought lakshmi-ganesh idols! There was just an apple and two laddus to appease and offer the gods for 'prasad'.

November Month

In all the good and bad moods and feelings I experience any day you are present. I wonder if I had any other constant relationship in my life except my father and mother! Like seasons, like the turning of the wind, people have twisted and turned. I know that "people are neither good nor bad, they are just different from our expectations." The same person is good, very good, for someone and on the other hand he is a terrible worst person for someone else! How to differentiate? How to make a judgment? I really can't understand human behavior which can change colors faster than a monitor lizard. We both brother-sister were different species, probably... remained the same through all rough and fair weather with human or animal behaved constant. The strangest encounter we faced were that suddenly some or the other closest and dearest people would stop talking for days, months, years and we would keep praying that good sense prevails and that he or she can clear the misunderstanding developed against us, meanwhile we would suffer more because that other person was in terrible state due to non-communication with us. I think '***Simplicity is Spirituality***'. And, in this complicated and fake world, Simplicity is the biggest misunderstood thing. Shailesh was by default spiritual. The harsh pilgrimages he undertook beginning right at tender age and continued till he departed was just a small reflection of his deep belief in spirituality and the Master of this creation, the Supreme Creator! When he carried the "*kaanvar yaatraa*" to Babadhaam (Deoghar), he never worried of the sore feet ambushed all over with numerous thorns and stones on the way and the bleeding and sore feet could never become a hindrance in completing the journey to reach his supreme God's abode. Lord Shiva was perpetually by his side, within him, all around him, he believed. He said that his name Shailesh is also a resonance of his Lord Shiva. He smiled at the deepest pains he was inflicted in his life. Brave, courageous, outstandingly lovable person, dangerously honest being. He was a king, an emperor of so many challenges and victories made him stronger and all the more courageous than before! December 2013 he took his family for a trip to Puri and I got the opportunity to join along. His knowledge, his grace, patience, his management skills were all exemplary. I wished to sit along him my whole life and learn so many things from him. The biggest thing however he taught was how to love all; from mass to class each and every category of people.

Jan 2022

Today Shailesh's little niece whom he teasingly called "Jhingri" (little prawn) who is just a five-year old cute kid has gone out with her parents to make her passport. Passport!...And I instantly remembered that Shailesh was the first person in our entire family (both paternal and maternal) to first think big and ventured out to make his passport without the support and encouragement of anyone. I asked my little niece Atishishti,- why do you wish to have a passport? And pat came her reply-"because I wish to roam about the whole world, see many places, meet the fairies as well as listen to stories of zombies, bask in the sands of sea beaches gathering a lot of shells, enjoy the huge mountains and splash in the fresh waterfalls, etc." ... which was what exactly Shailesh dreamt of. Sadly enough, he never ever got the opportunity to use his passport in his lifetime. When his son excelled in school studies and made his aim to become a scientist at NASA, United States of America, he used to say that all my troubles will be over once my son gets settled. Then I shall be able to fulfill all my dreams! His close friend Chakravarthy was one with whom he wished to live in an Ashram together in his old age.

He hated to be sick and never ever did he wish to get admitted in a hospital. At the most he visited the medical shop and used to bring some normal pills and medicines whenever he felt seriously in trouble, although for all the family members since childhood he had been through the hospitalization troubles and task doing forever. The last week of his life when he became so weak and his weight reduced drastically, his wife admitted him to hospital forcefully against his wishes. Although until he had strength he resisted his hospitalization. The worst fears came true and hospital bed took his life ultimately.

CHAPTER FIVE

ORDINARY YET EXTRAORDINARY

This memoir is not only dedicated to my brother's soul but a tribute to all those departed souls who left this worldly place unexpectedly and who were fill of numerous unrealized dreams and goals. I am not talking about greed, lustful ambitions or desires of human which have an infinite nature. I mean the basic necessities required for a bare minimum simple human life. I still keep wondering and questioning my existence as well as the existence of all sorts of life on this planet Earth. What is the real purpose of each soul here? Where is that knowledge that enlightens and the resilience and will power to conduct our lives according to the knowledge? How can we live successfully?

How can we live happily? Does Death take away all our pains, sorrows and negativity and washes away all our sins and wrong deeds?

I have realized that in life extraordinary souls live ordinary life. Wealth, money, property and assets are the power tools which can uplift ordinary souls and place them on the top hierarchy of society and when these are further powered with skills, talent and deep insight and knowledge,

such a soul is truly powerful. In spite of these crude facts, there are still a very little number of people who honor righteous virtues and conduct and behavior as the topmost value above money. As is said, things which money can't buy. As we progress towards the computer and super computer era, we are made to believe that there's nothing you cannot buy with wealth yet we have not been able to conquer Death with all our wealth! Wealth can only repair the damages for a while, or like is said,
"buy some more time
" for the rich and accelerate the death of poor due to unaffordable medical care- that's it!

I think *life is passion* and any compassionate soul to me seems to be one of the wealthiest people on earth. So when you have no material wealth, at least empower yourself with emotion and compassion. *Lend a smile to a sad soul even if you have no reason to smile for yourself.* Extend your hand to a needy even if no one ever has reached out to help you. Don't clinch your fists, open out your fingers and hearts! Life is passion. Humanity is compassion. Be Human, born as human beings. Do good karma and add value to your human birth. We are no ordinary souls but special creations of the Almighty. Hence live life extraordinary! That is what Shailesh taught everyone he happened to meet. He set an example to many ordinary thinking souls.

CHAPTER SIX

THE CAGED (FREE)SOUL

October 2022

Memories of Shailesh have been integrated into the entire ecosystem. All around me there are so many examples of creatures roaming freely in nature fighting for their survival and safety from other predators the birds, the lizards, the glow-worms and other insects and the goat and sheep to the lions and tiger. Their lives are full of struggles, yet they never go into depression. But human beings are experts in depression. One reason for this depression is "memories". That means we all are caged souls acting to be free and liberated. The fact is that we are never free of negative thoughts, emotions, sadness and therefore, depression. It is so difficult to be happy for us. All our education and knowledge fails us to make us strong enough to face certain events like death of a loved one. Our spirit is bounded by innumerable ties and we all, in real are like a caged soul trapped in our own physical bodies.

The Queen of Death is then like a boon which comes to liberate our souls from this cage to make us free soul. That is why the divine smile could be seen when Shailesh met

Lady Death and he jubilated ultimately that his caged soul was free after such a long yearning.

Before he left his body, he wasn't free; caged by his responsibilities of family, his children, wife, sisters, brother etc. He was least prepared to leave and depart all of a sudden from his dream abode 'Akinchan Kunj' which he had built stone by stone into a lovely house with all his heart and he was the reason why the simple house in a posh neighborhood was the centre of all the fun and frolic and festivities. He was celebration, he was jubilation himself! There were many rich and effluent homes but no one had such a warm and big heart like him. Circumstances and time compel nature for certain adaptations but there are some who decide to die if they have to almost reverse their God-given nature but they are never ever comfortable to change their garbs when their surroundings and environment change. Like suppose if a friend cheated him, he should have also turned him down the next time he asked for help; but No- not at all! Even understanding of the other person's intentions and nature of betrayal, Shailesh' soul would still motivate him to help that person whenever he seek help. That was Shailesh!

Six months before he died he was switching over the retired mode but yet couldn't entrust anyone completely to look after "Akinchan Kunj". He was not listened to, or understood by anyone and so he had withdrawn from all. Yet few regular friends visited him for their cup of tea and advice from him. He did communicate with me most of the time, yet sometimes he kept things to himself. Only the positive feelings he would share, I could sense his pain but helplessly was unable to remove them. I guess his pain was becoming unbearable. God, whom he always prayed to, had to answer his prayers. The caged soul had to be free! ...

Now our hands are empty. We are in chains. Our souls are tied to the *'Maya'(lust)* of this world. He is free! May his soul be free so. He deserved that freedom of happiness right here on earth for all the good deeds and love he generated to all. My prayers are for each one of us to attain liberty of our souls even when we are alive. That could be only happening when there is love, love and love in the world we live. Let us be more affectionate and loving and pray for all good liberated souls for effective guidance to lead a better, lovable, lives and not be 'caged'. Love you Brother Shailesh forever!

Photographic Memories Of Shailesh

Shailesh (Bhai Mama) with little niece Atishishti in front of Akinchan Kunj, Dhanbad.

Shailesh with his loving son Mist on the sands of Puri beach 2013.

Shailesh and Shipra during Diwali 2019

Bhai-Dooj festival 2019

Our loving parents (Papa& Maa)

Temple visit on his last birthday 2020

Devghar Oct 2020

When little sis bought her SUV car

Sailesh, Papa,Sashish(little brother)

Tarapeeth visit when his twin daughters were just one month old.

Loved little bro's daughter more than his own

Mother's hope and support

The family man (wife and three kids)

At Maithon Kalyaneshwari temple (niece' ceremony)

Shehenshah-bhai

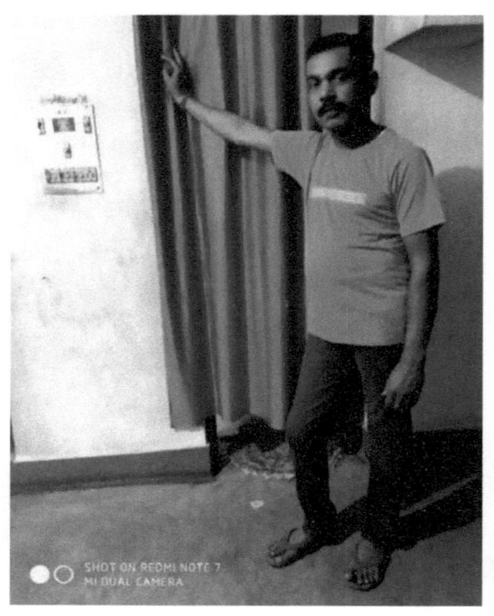

Losing weight yet strong-willed

Enter Caption

April 2021 remembering Shailesh after an year of his demise with his young kids

A Few Last Words

My sisters and brother reiterate:

I have not spent a single day since you left us when I may have missed to remember you. I cannot see you anymore;

Cannot listen you anymore,

But can feel your presence so strongly,

As if you are besides me forever!

You are always guiding me and showing me the right path to progress and prosper in life, overcoming the emotions, the pain, the stress that life has given and helping me to become a stronger and generous person.

I pray to almighty to keep my brother in peace now. (Shikha Tejswi)

Shubhra and Sashish have to grow and act as the eldest by default. There is no elder brother who could even take the roles of father and mother together. We move on in life with the presence of your lluminescence, carry on to spread the light of knowledge and the treasure of emotional love that we have inherited from you. His friends feel how incapacitated they've become now in spite of their millions of dollars earned. They've lost a genuine friend, philosopher and guide, a person who was happy in their progress, growth and development. Others who knew him miss for the number of times he had saved them during a personal crisis and upheld their social reputation.

I'm sure he must have been assigned a much greater and bigger role by the Supreme God wherever he has been taken away to, because the knowledge and good deeds never die and can never be erased. I have, in fact, envisioned this during my dreams and meditation that he is now happy where he is and carrying on his next assigned role with all his sincerity and dedication. He was a special and trustworthy person anyone could depend upon. Therefore, such souls are rare in this world and much in demand. So, they have to do a lot of service in a very short time and then they have to move on to other realms, I suppose. Good souls have a very short visa to this earth! Now you leave us with your memories and twinkle like a bright star in the dark, eerie Amavasya nights! Be our guiding star in our lives, dear Shailesh!

This book or **memoir** *was my small and desperate attempt to draw the sketch of a smart yet simple, ordinary- yet extraordinary soul who was so close to me for half a century. I wish that this simple story reaches out to all those living souls present in the world for the reason that we are able to transform and enlighten ourselves before we see any other soul depart from this temporary field of earth. Let us raise our consciousness and awaken to learn that each life is precious; every soul is special. Let us not abstain from our duties and fulfilling each life with love, care and humility of our service. For the crude fact that whatever we can do, can only be done when we have this instrument of our physical bodies. Our good deeds can add value and abundance to the lives of many and we have the power to create happiness through our good behavior and honest thoughts and the purest emotion of true love. A world so divine where traversing would be so comfortable. No soul shall be ever depressed when they are alive or even when it is time for them to leave this earth and travel to some other realms of the universe/multiverse. I hope with this memoir I have not hurt anybody's heart as all the living characters are very special dear ones to me close to my heart and I cannot even imagine intending any bad intention or feeling towards them even in the wildest of my dreams. More so, if I hurt them I would, in fact be hurting my loving departed brother Shailesh, who is the real motivation behind this whole book. I would like to admit honestly that many a time I have been* *drowned in a volley of emotions and many times I have slipped into bad words and moods and have almost leaked out my raw sentimental profile in this book, but I think that was necessary to pen down a true memoir. Once again I wish to convey lots of love to my dear brother whose memories will be always cherished. Thanks to all you constantly stayed by my side to help me overcome the pain and live a normal live once again. Thanks!*

Shipra Verma
Nov. 24th, 2022
Saharsa, Bihar.

यहीं, यहीं पर था जसिका एक आशयिाना
जमाने भर से सदा नभिाता था जो याराना
नज़र बुरी, जमाने की, उस पर सदा रही
तलि- तलि कर मारना पड़ा उसे ज़दिंगी

‘ए गम-ेदलि क्या करूँ, रो-रो मारा वो दीवाना
कहता रहा उसी और बहुत से वादे को है नभिाना
सब ठगते रहे, भोला था वो, था बड़ा दलिवाला
यम आये, कहा, “चल ये जग तेरा नहीं ठकिाना”।

(Dedicated to Shailesh)
Shipra Verma

About The Author

Shipra Verma is a Masters in Botany and a poet at heart writing poetry since childhood. A passionate music lover and singing is her life. She has been publishing her poems in magazines and digital media, also broadcasting on All India Radio, Mumbai and television. She writes in both Hindi and English and is equally apt in poetry as well as prose. Some of her creations are:- "Ravine and Peak (2018)English Poetry, Chhappan Bhog (2019), joint collection of Hindi Poems, Akinchan Kavitaayein (2005), and Intertwined Threads (2022), collection of short stories by several authors. She has also worked as an Editor for scientific magazines. A freelance Translator, she has translated many works into English from Hindi; Draupadi (by Sumitra Agrawal), Malavgadh ki Malvika (Santosh Srivastav), Hawwa ki beti (Divya Jain)...to name a few. She is currently translating Santosh Srivastav's novel 'Kathreen and life of Naga Sadhus' into English from Hindi.*

Post corona period she is migrated to her home town in Bihar and joined the department of Biotechnology at the prestigious MLT Saharsa College, Saharsa. Her writings usually are of the philosophical nature, emotionally charged, natural, with straight connect to the heart.

9 798888 834145

Printed by Libri Plureos GmbH in Hamburg,
Germany